COOKBOOK

50 UNIQUE AND EASY TOFU RECIPES

By
BookSumo Press
Copyright © 2015 by Saxonberg Associates
All rights reserved

Published by
BookSumo, a division of Saxonberg Associates
http://www.booksumo.com/

INTRODUCTION

Welcome to *The Effortless Chef Series*! Thank you for taking the time to download the *Easy Tofu Cookbook*. Come take a journey with me into the delights of easy cooking. The point of this cookbook and all my cookbooks is to exemplify the effortless nature of cooking simply.

In this book we focus on Tofu. You will find that even though the recipes are simple, the taste of the dishes is quite amazing.

So will you join me in an adventure of simple cooking? If the answer is yes (and I hope it is) please consult the table of contents to find the dishes you are most interested in. Once you are ready jump right in and start cooking.

Table of Contents

Introduction 2
Table of Contents 3
Legal Notes 7
Common Abbreviations 8
Chapter 1: All About Tofu 9
    The Chinese Origins of Tofu and Its Mysterious Nature 9
    A Nutritional Powerhouse 10
    Keeping Your Tofu As Fresh As Possible 11
    Soft and Firm. What This Means, and Why it Matters 12
    The Tofu Secret and Its Infinite Tastes 13
    The Fun of Cooking Tofu 14
    A Few Details on Cooking Tofu Properly.. 15
Chapter 2: Easy Tofu Recipes 18

Coconut Curry and Lemon Grass Tofu 18
(Thai Style) 18
Tomato Parmesan, and Mozzarella Tofu 22
Sweet Curry and Ginger Tofu 25
Lasagna 28
Zucchini and Lime Tofu 31
Southeast Asian Tofu with Broccoli 34
Vietnamese Tofu 37
Tofu Burgers 41
Italian Herbed Tofu Soup 44
Maple Syrup and Hot Sauce Tofu Bites 47
Sweet and Sour Tofu 50
Garbanzos and Basil Tofu 53
Easy BBQ Tofu 56
Easy BBQ Tofu II 59
Orange Chili Carrot Tofu 62
Rustic Tofu 65
Cheddar Tofu Quiche I 68

Celery Tofu Salad 71
Creamy Asiago Tofu 74
Mexican Style Tofu 77
Lasagna II 80
(Vegan Approved) 80
Sweet Tofu Stir Fry 84
American Style Tofu 88
Tofu Pudding 91
Indian Style Tofu 93
Cilantro and Sesame Tofu 96
Tofu Party Dip 99
3 Cheese Tofu Pasta Shells 101
Cranberry, Pecan, and Pepper Tofu 105
German Style tofu 109
Mushrooms and Pasta Tofu 112
Choco Tofu Pie 115
Easy Asian Tofu 118
Tofu Salad II 120
Triple Tofu Quiche II 123
Peppers and Mozzarella Tofu 126

Indian Style Tofu II 129
Rice and Spinach Tofu 132
Peanut Butter and Ginger Tofu 135
Easy Japanese Style Tofu 138
Tofu Chili 140
Taiwanese Style Tofu 143
Tofu Tartar Sandwich 146
Caribbean Style Tofu 149
Easy Tofu Cheesecake 152
Ranch and Spinach Tofu 155
Indian Style Tofu III 158
California Style Tofu 162
Olives and Soy Sauce Tofu 165
Pad Thai Noodles 168

THANKS FOR READING! NOW LET'S TRY SOME **SUSHI** AND **DUMP DINNERS** 172

LEGAL NOTES

ALL RIGHTS RESERVED. NO PART OF THIS BOOK MAY BE REPRODUCED OR TRANSMITTED IN ANY FORM OR BY ANY MEANS. PHOTOCOPYING, POSTING ONLINE, AND / OR DIGITAL COPYING IS STRICTLY PROHIBITED UNLESS WRITTEN PERMISSION IS GRANTED BY THE BOOK'S PUBLISHING COMPANY. LIMITED USE OF THE BOOK'S TEXT IS PERMITTED FOR USE IN REVIEWS WRITTEN FOR THE PUBLIC AND/OR PUBLIC DOMAIN.

COMMON ABBREVIATIONS

cup(s)	C.
tablespoon	tbsp
teaspoon	tsp
ounce	oz.
pound	lb

*All units used are standard American measurements

Chapter 1: All About Tofu

The Chinese Origins of Tofu and Its Mysterious Nature

Tofu is as Chinese as Chinese New Year. Meaning it is very Chinese.

What we know, for a fact, is that Tofu originated in China.

Tofu is savored all over China and also many parts of South East Asia.

Tofu production is extremely ancient and was very popular in China during the early dynasties. But we DO NOT know its EXACT origins.

There are many folktales about the origin of Tofu production but none have been proven.

Sadly tofu is like many other culinary classics like cheese and butter. Staple foods we take for granted, but do not know their origins.

So when you eat tofu, or you eat cheese, or use some butter, remember the following fact:

To this day, we have no real historical understanding of their exact origins or who came up with their production techniques!

Overall, tofu is one of the most versatile non-meat protein sources in the grocery store.

It is also one of the most nutritious low calorie options for anyone who cares about making every calorie of their food count.

A NUTRITIONAL POWERHOUSE

Tofu has 8 essential amino acids and a ton of protein.

In fact, according to the FDA 25 grams of tofu, daily, can possibly lower your risk for heart disease.

Tofu also contains absolutely no cholesterol!

Again, tofu contains absolutely no cholesterol.

There aren't many foods which have no cholesterol, but tofu is one.

Therefore, if you happen to have high cholesterol consider replacing the meat in some of your meals with tofu.

One serving of tofu is about half of a cup or 4.5 ounces.

Eating this exact amount of tofu will provide: 20% of your daily protein needs, 43% of your calcium needs, and 36% of the iron your body needs each day.

Can you see why tofu is one of healthiest foods you can consume? It contains no cholesterol, hardly any fat, and very minimal calories. Yet it still delivers the nutrients!

KEEPING YOUR TOFU AS FRESH AS POSSIBLE

Tofu will last about 2 to 3 months if frozen.

If you open the package and expose the tofu to air it, will last only for a day or so if you do not change the water.

If you change the water surrounding the tofu daily, it will last for 3 to 4 days, while refrigerated.

It is very important to note this fact:

Do not let your uncooked tofu sit exposed to air. Always refrigerate it. If you buy large amounts of tofu, keep them frozen in the freezer.

Frozen tofu is good for up to 3 months (which is a long time).

Once you open a pack of tofu and thaw it be ready to cook it within a few hours!

SOFT AND FIRM. WHAT THIS MEANS, AND WHY IT MATTERS

When buying tofu there will almost always be two choices: soft and firm.

The difference between the choices relates to the amount of water that has been removed before the tofu was packed.

Soft tofu lends itself best for applications where it would be crumbled.

Such as over a salad.

The firm type of tofu is good for being cut, sliced, and diced. Firm tofu is best for stir frying, baking, pan frying, and deep frying.

THE TOFU SECRET AND ITS INFINITE TASTES

Have you ever wondered why tofu is always full of water? Well the reason for this is due to the nature of the proteins which make up the tofu.

Normal "firm tofu" also called "Chinese tofu", is very similar to a sponge. Meaning, tofu will absorb any liquid that surrounds it!

Understanding this fact, that tofu will absorb anything that it is placed in, can yield some interesting tastes and dishes.

Tofu is not bland.

In fact, it has an infinite number of unique tastes. This is because you can marinate your tofu in an infinite number of ways.

Remember, tofu is essentially a sponge and it will soak up any liquid that it is placed in.

Once these liquids have been absorbed, and the tofu is cooked, you will taste the marinade.

THE FUN OF COOKING TOFU

So maybe you love the taste of oranges, or cranberries.

Try marinating your tofu in some fresh orange or cranberry juice for 15 mins. Then fry it.

Your tofu will have a subtle but noticeable fruity taste.

The possibilities are absolutely infinite, and this is where the fun of cooking tofu begins, when you start to experiment with different tastes and marinades.

Some ideas include: Worcestershire sauce, Steak sauce, soy sauce, orange juice, cranberry juice, broth, hoisin sauce, liquid smoke, fish sauce, etc.

But let's talk about a few more things related to cooking tofu and tapping into this secret nature of infinite tastes.

A Few Details on Cooking Tofu Properly

First and foremost, before you marinate a block of tofu make sure you slice the block into smaller pieces. You can also cut the tofu into cubes.

Try cutting the block of tofu into thin slices, or slice the entire block into 4 slabs.

Cutting the tofu in this manner will make it easier to marinate.

Once you have sliced the tofu into more manageable pieces it is important to remove the water the tofu has absorbed from its packaging.

The easiest way to do this is to cover your tofu in some paper towels and place the wrapped tofu on a cutting board.

Lay a cookie sheet over the covered pieces of tofu and place something heavy on the cookie sheet, like a skillet.

Let the tofu sit under the skillet for an hour.

By removing these extra liquids you are making space for the marinade. The more liquid you remove, the more space there is for extra marinade, and the tastier your tofu will be.

One of the best ways to cook marinated tofu is to pan fry it.

When pan frying tofu, first coat your pieces with flour lightly, then with whisked eggs.

After doing this your pieces of tofu are ready for hot oil.

Try using different types of oils like sesame, coconut, peanut, or olive oil for even more unique tastes!

Fry the pieces of tofu until they are slightly brown and crisp on both sides and that's it.

So now that we understand a lot about Tofu, its Chinese nature, the nutritional facts, its proper storage, and how to unlock its infinite tastes let's dive into some recipes.

The first recipe we shall learn is from Thailand and it's a delicious coconut curry tofu that you will absolutely love.

Chapter 2: Easy Tofu Recipes

Coconut Curry and Lemon Grass Tofu

(Thai Style)

Ingredients

- 1 (14 oz.) can coconut milk
- 2 C. vegetable broth
- 1 (1 inch) piece galangal
- 2 stalks lemon grass, bruised and chopped
- 5 kaffir lime leaves, torn
- 1/2 tsp Thai red curry paste
- 1 (12 oz.) package extra firm tofu, drained and cubed
- 1/2 C. stemmed and sliced shiitake mushrooms
- 1/2 C. sliced button mushrooms
- 2 tbsps fresh lime juice

- 2 1/2 tbsps brown sugar
- 1/8 tsp turmeric powder
- 4 oz. dry rice stick noodles
- 1/2 tsp crushed red pepper flakes

Directions

- Get the following boiling for 2 mins: kaffir leaves, coconut milk, lemon grass, galangal, and broth.
- Once everything is boiling lower the heat to a gentle simmer.
- Let the mix simmer for 17 mins.
- Now run the mix through a strainer and keep only the liquid, throw away anything else.
- Add the broth back to the pot and also add in: turmeric, curry paste, brown sugar, tofu, lime juice, button and shiitake mushrooms.
- Get the contents lightly boiling again and continue cooking for 12 mins.
- Simultaneously get your rice noodles boiling in water and salt.

- Boil this mix for 5 mins then remove all the liquids.
- Divide the noodles between your serving bowls and top everything with a good amount of broth mix.
- Add some more pepper flakes as well.
- Enjoy.

Amount per serving (4 total)

Timing Information:

Preparation	30 m
Cooking	30 m
Total Time	1 h

Nutritional Information:

Calories	434 kcal
Fat	25.7 g
Carbohydrates	43.7g
Protein	12.7 g
Cholesterol	0 mg
Sodium	269 mg

* Percent Daily Values are based on a 2,000 calorie diet.

Tomato Parmesan, and Mozzarella Tofu

Ingredients

- 1/2 C. seasoned bread crumbs
- 5 tbsps grated Parmesan cheese
- 2 tsps dried oregano, divided
- salt to taste
- ground black pepper to taste
- 1 (12 oz.) package firm tofu, cut into 1/4 inch slices
- 2 tbsps olive oil
- 1 (8 oz.) can tomato sauce
- 1/2 tsp dried basil
- 1 clove garlic, minced
- 4 oz. shredded mozzarella cheese

Directions

- Get a bowl, mix: black pepper, bread crumbs, salt, parmesan (2 tbsps), and half of the oregano.

- Get a 2nd bowl, mix: oregano, tomato sauce, garlic, and basil.
- Place your cut tofu, into some cool water, in a bowl, now coat each piece of tofu with the dry parmesan mix.
- Set your oven to 400 degrees before doing anything else.
- Fry each piece of tofu in olive oil until browned and slightly crispy on both sides.
- Layer all your tofu pieces into a casserole dish and top with the tomato mix and finally a layer of mozzarella and the rest of the parmesan.
- Cook everything in the oven for 25 mins.
- Enjoy.

Amount per serving (4 total)

Timing Information:

Preparation	25 m
Cooking	20 m
Total Time	45 m

Nutritional Information:

Calories	357 kcal
Fat	21.5 g
Carbohydrates	18.8g
Protein	25.7 g
Cholesterol	24 mg
Sodium	841 mg

* Percent Daily Values are based on a 2,000 calorie diet.

Sweet Curry and Ginger Tofu

Ingredients

- 2 bunches green onions
- 1 (14 oz.) can light coconut milk
- 1/4 C. soy sauce, divided
- 1/2 tsp brown sugar
- 1 1/2 tsps curry powder
- 1 tsp minced fresh ginger
- 2 tsps chili paste
- 1 lb firm tofu, cut into 3/4 inch cubes
- 4 roma (plum) tomatoes, chopped
- 1 yellow bell pepper, thinly sliced
- 4 oz. fresh mushrooms, chopped
- 1/4 C. chopped fresh basil
- 4 C. chopped bok choy
- salt to taste

Directions

- Separate the green portion of the onions and dice it into 2" pieces.
- Now get the following boiling: chili paste, coconut milk, ginger, 3 tbsps soy sauce, curry, and brown sugar.
- Once everything is boiling add in: mushrooms, tofu, onions, yellow pepper, and tomatoes.
- Place a lid on the pot and let it all cook for 7 mins, then add in bok choy, pepper, salt, the rest of the soy sauce, and the basil.
- Cook the contents for 7 more mins then add the rest of the onions.
- Enjoy.

Amount per serving (6 total)

Timing Information:

Preparation	25 m
Cooking	15 m
Total Time	40 m

Nutritional Information:

Calories	232 kcal
Fat	13.2 g
Carbohydrates	16.9g
Protein	16.5 g
Cholesterol	0 mg
Sodium	680 mg

* Percent Daily Values are based on a 2,000 calorie diet.

Lasagna

Ingredients

- 1/2 (12 oz.) package uncooked lasagna noodles
- 1 (12 oz.) package firm tofu, crumbled
- 2 eggs
- 1/4 tsp salt
- 1/4 tsp black pepper
- 1/4 tsp ground nutmeg
- 2 tbsps milk
- 1 C. spaghetti sauce
- 1 tbsp dried parsley
- 2 C. shredded mozzarella cheese, divided
- 1/2 C. grated Parmesan cheese

Directions

- Set your oven to 350 degrees before doing anything else.

- Get a bowl, combine: 1 C. mozzarella, tofu, parsley, eggs, pasta sauce, salt, milk, nutmeg, and pepper.
- Boil your noodles in water and salt for 9 mins, then remove all the liquids.
- Cover the bottom of a casserole dish with some noodles, then, some of the tomato sauce mix, more noodles, and finally more sauce.
- Continue until all the ingredients have been used. Top the lasagna with parmesan and mozzarella.
- Cook the layers, for 30 mins, in the oven.
- Enjoy.

Amount per serving (7 total)

Timing Information:

Preparation	20 m
Cooking	35 m
Total Time	55 m

Nutritional Information:

Calories	324 kcal
Fat	14.5 g
Carbohydrates	26.2g
Protein	24.1 g
Cholesterol	81 mg
Sodium	569 mg

* Percent Daily Values are based on a 2,000 calorie diet.

Zucchini and Lime Tofu

Ingredients

- 2 tbsps peanut oil
- 1 (16 oz.) package extra-firm tofu, cut into bite-sized cubes
- 1 tbsp minced fresh ginger root
- 2 tbsps red curry paste
- 1 lb zucchini, diced
- 1 red bell pepper, diced
- 3 tbsps lime juice
- 3 tbsps soy sauce
- 2 tbsps maple syrup
- 1 (14 oz.) can coconut milk
- 1/2 C. chopped fresh basil

Directions

- Stir fry your tofu in peanut oil until browned all over. Then the tofu place to the side.

- Add the curry paste and ginger into the oil and cook them for 30 secs while stirring.
- Now add the bell peppers and the zucchini.
- Stir fry the veggies for 60 secs then add: tofu, lime juice, coconut milk, soy sauce, and syrup.
- Get everything gently boiling for 2 mins then then add some basil and shut the heat.
- Enjoy.

Amount per serving (4 total)

Timing Information:

Preparation	20 m
Cooking	10 m
Total Time	30 m

Nutritional Information:

Calories	425 kcal
Fat	38.8 g
Carbohydrates	20.9g
Protein	18.4 g
Cholesterol	0 mg
Sodium	856 mg

* Percent Daily Values are based on a 2,000 calorie diet.

Southeast Asian Tofu with Broccoli

Ingredients

- 1 tbsp peanut oil
- 1 small head broccoli, chopped
- 1 small red bell pepper, chopped
- 5 fresh mushrooms, sliced
- 1 lb firm tofu, cubed
- 1/2 C. peanut butter
- 1/2 C. hot water
- 2 tbsps vinegar
- 2 tbsps soy sauce
- 1 1/2 tbsps molasses
- ground cayenne pepper to taste

Directions

- Get a bowl, mix the following, until smooth: cayenne, peanut butter, molasses, hot water, soy sauce, and vinegar.

- Stir fry your tofu, broccoli, mushrooms, and bell peppers in the oil for 7 mins.
- Add in the peanut mix and cook for 6 more mins with a gentle boil.
- Enjoy.

Amount per serving (4 total)

Timing Information:

Preparation	10 m
Cooking	10 m
Total Time	20 m

Nutritional Information:

Calories	443 kcal
Fat	29.9 g
Carbohydrates	24g
Protein	29 g
Cholesterol	0 mg
Sodium	641 mg

* Percent Daily Values are based on a 2,000 calorie diet.

Vietnamese Tofu

Ingredients

- 2 tbsps vegetable oil
- 1 onion, coarsely chopped
- 2 shallots, thinly sliced
- 2 cloves garlic, chopped
- 2 inch piece fresh ginger root, thinly sliced
- 1 stalk lemon grass, cut into 2 inch pieces
- 4 tbsps curry powder
- 1 green bell pepper, coarsely chopped
- 2 carrots, peeled and diagonally sliced
- 8 mushrooms, sliced
- 1 lb fried tofu, cut into bite-size pieces
- 4 C. vegetable broth
- 4 C. water
- 2 tbsps vegetarian fish sauce (optional)
- 2 tsps red pepper flakes

- 1 bay leaf
- 2 kaffir lime leaves
- 8 small potatoes, quartered
- 1 (14 oz.) can coconut milk
- 2 C. fresh bean sprouts, for garnish
- 8 sprigs fresh chopped cilantro, for garnish

Directions

- Stir fry your shallots and onions in oil until the onions are see-through then add in: curry, garlic, lemon grass, and ginger.
- Stir fry everything for about 6 more mins then add: tofu, green peppers, mushrooms, and carrots.
- Cook the mix for 2 more mins before adding in the veggie stock, pepper flakes, and fish sauce.
- Stir everything and get it all boiling.

- Once the contents are boiling add in the coconut milk and the potatoes, get it all boiling again.
- Once the soup is boiling set the heat to low and let the mix gently cook for 50 mins.
- When serving the soup top it with some fresh cilantro and some bean sprouts.
- Enjoy.

Amount per serving (8 total)

Timing Information:

Preparation	30 m
Cooking	1 h 30 m
Total Time	2 h

Nutritional Information:

Calories	479 kcal
Fat	26.5 g
Carbohydrates	51.4g
Protein	16.4 g
Cholesterol	0 mg
Sodium	271 mg

* Percent Daily Values are based on a 2,000 calorie diet.

Tofu Burgers

Ingredients

- 1 (12 oz.) package firm tofu
- 2 tsps vegetable oil
- 1 small onion, chopped
- 1 celery, chopped
- 1 egg, beaten
- 1/4 C. shredded Cheddar cheese
- salt and pepper to taste
- 1/2 C. vegetable oil for frying

Directions

- Let your tofu sit in the freezer for 2 days before doing anything else.
- Once the tofu is completely frozen drop the package into some simmering water for 22 mins.
- Stir fry your celery and onions in 2 tsps of veggie oil, until

- browned, and then pour everything into a bowl.
- After the tofu is no longer frozen, press out the water, dice it, and add it with the onions.
- Also combine in: pepper, whisked eggs, salt, and cheese.
- Divide this mix into six parts.
- Heat half a C. of veggie oil then fry each of the 6 divided portions of the tofu and use a spatula to form them into burgers.
- Cook everything for about 6 mins then flip it and cook for 6 more mins.
- Enjoy.

Amount per serving (6 total)

Timing Information:

Preparation	40 m
Cooking	15 m
Total Time	3 d

Nutritional Information:

Calories	151 kcal
Fat	11 g
Carbohydrates	4.1g
Protein	11.3 g
Cholesterol	28 mg
Sodium	59 mg

* Percent Daily Values are based on a 2,000 calorie diet.

Italian Herbed Tofu Soup

Ingredients

- 2 tbsps butter
- 2 C. sliced carrots
- 1 1/2 C. chopped onion
- 1 1/2 C. chopped celery
- 1 1/2 tsps minced garlic
- 12 C. vegetarian chicken-flavored broth
- 2 C. egg noodles
- 1 (14 oz.) container extra-firm tofu, drained and cubed
- 1/4 C. raisins
- 1/2 tsp dried basil
- 1/2 tsp dried oregano
- 1/4 tsp poultry seasoning
- 1/4 tsp dried thyme
- 1/4 tsp dried rosemary
- 1/4 tsp dried marjoram
- 1/4 tsp black pepper
- 1/4 C. cornstarch
- 3 tbsps cold water

Directions

- Get a bowl, mix until smooth: water and cornstarch.
- Stir fry the following in butter for 12 mins: garlic, carrots, celery, and onions.
- Now add in the broth and get it all boiling.
- Once everything is boiling, add: pepper, noodles, marjoram, raisins, rosemary, basil, thyme, cornstarch mix, oregano, and poultry seasoning.
- Get the contents boiling again then place a lid on the pot, set the heat to low, and let it all gently cook for 35 mins.
- Enjoy.

Amount per serving (4 total)

Timing Information:

Preparation	15 m
Cooking	40 m
Total Time	55 m

Nutritional Information:

Calories	358 kcal
Fat	12.9 g
Carbohydrates	49g
Protein	17.1 g
Cholesterol	29 mg
Sodium	1484 mg

* Percent Daily Values are based on a 2,000 calorie diet.

Maple Syrup and Hot Sauce Tofu Bites

Ingredients

- 1 (16 oz.) package extra firm tofu, pressed and diced into cubes
- 1/4 C. soy sauce
- 2 tbsps maple syrup
- 2 tbsps ketchup
- 1 tbsp vinegar
- 1 dash hot sauce
- 1 tbsp sesame seeds
- 1/4 tsp garlic powder
- 1/4 tsp ground black pepper
- 1 tsp liquid smoke flavoring

Directions

- Coat a casserole dish with nonstick spray and then set your oven to 375 degrees before doing anything else.

- Get a bowl, combine: hot sauce, sesame seeds, soy sauce, tofu cubes, garlic powder, vinegar, black pepper, ketchup, liquid smoke, and syrup.
- Toss the mixture to evenly coat all the tofu pieces. Place a covering on the bowl and let it sit for 30 mins. Now pour the tofu pieces and their sauce into the casserole dish and cook in the oven for 17 mins then flip the tofu pieces and continue cooking for 12 more mins.
- Enjoy.

Amount per serving (4 total)

Timing Information:

Preparation	10 m
Cooking	15 m
Total Time	25 m

Nutritional Information:

Calories	168 kcal
Fat	8.8 g
Carbohydrates	12.8g
Protein	12.7 g
Cholesterol	0 mg
Sodium	1002 mg

* Percent Daily Values are based on a 2,000 calorie diet.

Sweet and Sour Tofu

Ingredients

- 3 tbsps peanut oil
- 1 lb firm tofu, cubed
- 1 red onion, sliced
- 1 red bell pepper, sliced
- 1 green chili pepper, chopped
- 3 cloves garlic, crushed
- 1/3 C. hot water
- 3 tbsps white vinegar
- 3 tbsps soy sauce
- 1 tbsp brown sugar
- 1 tsp cornstarch
- 1 tsp crushed red pepper flakes

Directions

- Get a bowl, combine until smooth: red pepper flakes, hot water, cornstarch, vinegar, brown sugar, and soy sauce.

- Stir fry your tofu in peanut oil until browned all over then add in: garlic, onions, chili peppers, and bell peppers.
- Continue stir frying for 7 more mins.
- Now add in the wet mix and cook for 6 more mins until the mix becomes thicker.
- Enjoy.

Amount per serving (4 total)

Timing Information:

Preparation	10 m
Cooking	12 m
Total Time	22 m

Nutritional Information:

Calories	307 kcal
Fat	20.3 g
Carbohydrates	16.3g
Protein	19.7 g
Cholesterol	0 mg
Sodium	697 mg

* Percent Daily Values are based on a 2,000 calorie diet.

GARBANZOS AND BASIL TOFU

Ingredients

- 1 tbsp vegetable oil
- 1 onion, chopped
- 1 (14.75 oz.) can creamed corn
- 1 tbsp curry paste
- salt to taste
- ground black pepper to taste
- 1/2 tsp garlic powder, or to taste
- 1 (15 oz.) can garbanzo beans (chickpeas), drained and rinsed
- 1 (12 oz.) package firm tofu, cubed
- 1 bunch fresh spinach, stems removed
- 1 tsp dried basil or to taste

Directions

- Stir fry your onions until see-through and then add in: curry paste and cream corn.

- Stir fry the mix for 7 more mins then add: spinach, garlic, tofu, pepper, garbanzos, and salt.
- Place a lid on the pot and cook everything for 3 more mins before shutting the heat and adding in the basil.
- Enjoy.

Amount per serving (4 total)

Timing Information:

Preparation	5 m
Cooking	15 m
Total Time	20 m

Nutritional Information:

Calories	346 kcal
Fat	12.3 g
Carbohydrates	44.7g
Protein	21.7 g
Cholesterol	0 mg
Sodium	849 mg

* Percent Daily Values are based on a 2,000 calorie diet.

Easy BBQ Tofu

Ingredients

- 1 (16 oz.) package extra firm tofu, pressed, and cut into strips
- 3 tbsps olive oil
- 1 egg white
- 1 tbsp barbeque sauce
- 1 C. all-purpose flour
- 1 tsp salt
- 1/2 tsp pepper
- 1 C. barbeque sauce

Directions

- Freeze your sliced tofu throughout the night. Then thaw out the tofu and dry the pieces.
- Get a bowl, combine: 1 tbsp bbq sauce, and egg whites.
- Get a 2nd bowl, combine: pepper, flour, and salt.

- Get your olive oil hot, and turn on your broiler before doing anything else.
- Now coat your tofu with the egg and dry mix.
- Fry the pieces for 60 secs per side.
- Layer the tofu pieces in a broiler pan or dish and top everything with the rest of the bbq sauce.
- Cook the tofu pieces under the broiler for 6 mins per side.
- Enjoy with some more bbq sauce.

Amount per serving (4 total)

Timing Information:

Preparation	10 m
Cooking	25 m
Total Time	8 h 35 m

Nutritional Information:

Calories	409 kcal
Fat	17.2 g
Carbohydrates	50.4g
Protein	15.2 g
Cholesterol	0 mg
Sodium	1348 mg

* Percent Daily Values are based on a 2,000 calorie diet.

Easy BBQ Tofu II

Ingredients

- 1 (12 oz.) package extra firm tofu, pressed and drained, cut into 1/4 inch slices.
- 3 tbsps vegetable oil
- 1 onion, thinly sliced
- 1 1/2 C. barbecue sauce
- 6 hamburger buns

Directions

- Brown both sides of your tofu slices in veggie oil then add the onions and continue browning for about 7 more mins until the onions are soft.
- Add in the bbq sauce and cook the mix for 7 more mins with a low level of heat.
- Serve the tofu pieces on sesame seed buns.

- Enjoy.

Amount per serving (6 total)

Timing Information:

Preparation	5 m
Cooking	10 m
Total Time	15 m

Nutritional Information:

Calories	336 kcal
Fat	12.5 g
Carbohydrates	47.1g
Protein	9.4 g
Cholesterol	0 mg
Sodium	945 mg

* Percent Daily Values are based on a 2,000 calorie diet.

Orange Chili Carrot Tofu

Ingredients

- 1/4 C. vegetable oil for frying
- 1/4 C. cornstarch
- 1 (16 oz.) package firm tofu, drained and cut into strips
- 2 tbsps soy sauce
- 1/2 C. orange juice
- 1/4 C. warm water
- 1 tbsp sugar
- 1 tsp chili paste
- 1 tsp cornstarch
- 1 tbsp vegetable oil
- 2 carrots, sliced

Directions

- Get a bowl, combine: cornstarch (1 tsp), soy sauce, chili paste, orange juice, sugar, and water.
- Coat your tofu with 1/4 a C. of cornstarch then stir fry them in

1/4 a C. of oil for 7 mins, flipping half way.
- Now set everything to the side on some paper towels.
- Add in the rest of the oil and fry the carrots until they become soft.
- Add in the orange juice mix and get it all boiling.
- Once the contents are boiling add in the tofu and cook everything for 2 more mins before coating the pieces evenly.
- Enjoy.

Amount per serving (4 total)

Timing Information:

Preparation	15 m
Cooking	15 m
Total Time	30 m

Nutritional Information:

Calories	286 kcal
Fat	15 g
Carbohydrates	23.3g
Protein	18.9 g
Cholesterol	0 mg
Sodium	500 mg

* Percent Daily Values are based on a 2,000 calorie diet.

Rustic Tofu

Ingredients

- 1 (16 oz.) package extra-firm tofu, drained and pressed, cut into 1/2 inch slices, then cut again into 4 cubes
- 2 C. vegetable broth
- 3 tbsps vegetable oil
- 1/2 C. all-purpose flour
- 3 tbsps nutritional yeast
- 1 tsp salt
- 1/2 tsp freshly ground black pepper
- 1 tsp sage
- 1/2 tsp cayenne pepper

Directions

- Cover your tofu with broth in a bowl then let them sit submerged.

- Get a 2nd bowl, combine: cayenne, flour, sage, yeast, pepper, and salt.
- Dip your tofu pieces into the dry mix then fry them in hot oil until browned all over.
- Enjoy.

Amount per serving (4 total)

Timing Information:

Preparation	15 m
Cooking	15 m
Total Time	30 m

Nutritional Information:

Calories	285 kcal
Fat	17.5 g
Carbohydrates	18.9g
Protein	16.3 g
Cholesterol	0 mg
Sodium	823 mg

* Percent Daily Values are based on a 2,000 calorie diet.

Cheddar Tofu Quiche I

Ingredients

- 1 (8 oz.) container tofu
- 1/3 C. 1% milk
- 1/2 tsp salt, or to taste
- 1/2 tsp pepper
- 1 (10 oz.) package frozen chopped spinach, thawed and drained
- 1 tsp minced garlic
- 1/4 C. diced onion
- 2/3 C. shredded Cheddar cheese
- 1/2 C. shredded Swiss cheese
- 1 unbaked 9 inch pie crust

Directions

- Set your oven to 350 degrees before doing anything else.
- Puree the following in a blender: milk, pepper, salt, and tofu.

- Get a bowl, mix: tofu puree, spinach, Swiss, garlic, cheddar, and onions.
- Fill your crust with the mix and cook the contents in the oven for 35 mins.
- Enjoy.

Amount per serving (6 total)

Timing Information:

Preparation	15 m
Cooking	30 m
Total Time	45 m

Nutritional Information:

Calories	288 kcal
Fat	18.8 g
Carbohydrates	18.5g
Protein	12.7 g
Cholesterol	22 mg
Sodium	489 mg

* Percent Daily Values are based on a 2,000 calorie diet.

Celery Tofu Salad

Ingredients

- 2 tbsps mayonnaise
- 1 tbsp sweet pickle relish
- 1 tsp distilled white vinegar
- 1 tsp prepared mustard
- 1 tsp white sugar
- 1/2 tsp ground turmeric
- 1/4 tsp dried dill weed
- 1 tbsp dried parsley
- 1 lb firm tofu, sliced and well drained
- 1 tbsp minced onion
- 2 tbsps minced celery
- salt to taste
- ground black pepper to taste

Directions

- Get a bowl, mix: parsley, mayo, dill, relish, turmeric, vinegar, sugar, and mustard.

- Get a 2nd bowl, mashed together: celery, tofu, pepper, salt, and onions.
- Combine both bowls and add in some extra pepper and salt.
- Now place everything in the fridge until cold.
- Enjoy.

Amount per serving (4 total)

Timing Information:

Preparation	
Cooking	10 m
Total Time	4 h 10 m

Nutritional Information:

Calories	227 kcal
Fat	15.5 g
Carbohydrates	8.2g
Protein	18.2 g
Cholesterol	3 mg
Sodium	90 mg

* Percent Daily Values are based on a 2,000 calorie diet.

Creamy Asiago Tofu

Ingredients

- 1 tbsp butter
- 1 tbsp olive oil
- 1 small onion, chopped
- 2 cloves garlic, minced
- 2 lbs fresh spinach, washed and chopped
- 1 (12 oz.) package firm tofu
- 1/2 C. milk or soy milk
- 1 C. Asiago cheese
- garlic powder to taste
- salt and pepper to taste

Directions

- Puree the following in a blender: pepper, tofu, salt, cheese, and garlic.
- Stir fry your garlic and onions in olive oil and butter for about 5 mins until see-through.

- Now combine in the spinach for 3 more mins until tender and then add the puree.
- Cook the contents until hot for about 3 more mins.
- Top with asiago.
- Enjoy.

Amount per serving (8 total)

Timing Information:

Preparation	20 m
Cooking	10 m
Total Time	30 m

Nutritional Information:

Calories	152 kcal
Fat	9.5 g
Carbohydrates	7.3g
Protein	12.1 g
Cholesterol	16 mg
Sodium	301 mg

* Percent Daily Values are based on a 2,000 calorie diet.

Mexican Style Tofu

Ingredients

- 1 (16 oz.) package garden herb tofu, crumbled
- 2 tbsps vegetable oil
- 1 clove garlic, minced
- 1/2 C. chopped onion
- 2 tsps chili powder
- 1/4 tsp paprika
- 1/4 tsp cayenne pepper
- 1/4 tsp ground cumin
- 1/4 tsp salt
- 1/2 lime, juiced
- 1/2 C. tomato sauce
- 1/4 C. chopped fresh cilantro
- 10 medium taco shells, heated
- 2 C. shredded lettuce
- 2 tomatoes, chopped
- 1 avocado - peeled, pitted and diced
- 1 C. shredded Cheddar cheese
- 1/4 C. salsa

Directions

- For 7 mins stir fry your onions, garlic, and tofu in oil. Then combine in the tomato sauce, chili powder, lime juice, paprika, salt, cayenne, and cumin.
- Continue cooking for 5 more mins. Then add the cilantro.
- Fill your shells with the mix and then layer some salsa, lettuce, cheese, avocadoes, and tomatoes.
- Enjoy.

Amount per serving (8 total)

Timing Information:

Preparation	10 m
Cooking	40 m
Total Time	50 m

Nutritional Information:

Calories	278 kcal
Fat	18.3 g
Carbohydrates	20.2g
Protein	11 g
Cholesterol	15 mg
Sodium	382 mg

* Percent Daily Values are based on a 2,000 calorie diet.

Lasagna II

(Vegan Approved)

Ingredients

- 2 tbsps olive oil
- 1 1/2 C. chopped onion
- 3 tbsps minced garlic
- 4 (14.5 oz.) cans stewed tomatoes
- 1/3 C. tomato paste
- 1/2 C. chopped fresh basil
- 1/2 C. chopped parsley
- 1 tsp salt
- 1 tsp ground black pepper
- 1 (16 oz.) package lasagna noodles
- 2 lbs firm tofu
- 2 tbsps minced garlic
- 1/4 C. chopped fresh basil
- 1/4 C. chopped parsley
- 1/2 tsp salt
- ground black pepper to taste

- 3 (10 oz.) packages frozen chopped spinach, thawed and drained

Directions

- Stir fry your onions in olive oil for 7 mins then add in the garlic and cook for 7 more mins.
- Now add: parsley, tomatoes, pepper, salt, basil, and tomato paste.
- Get the mix boiling, then place a lid on the pot, and let the contents gently cook with a low level of heat for 65 mins.
- Simultaneously boil your noodles in water and salt for 9 mins. Then remove all the liquid.
- Get a bowl, mash: pepper, tofu, salt, garlic, parsley, and basil.
- Set your oven to 400 degrees before, doing anything else.
- Now get a baking dish and layer the following in it: noodles, 1/3

tofu mix, spinach, 1.5 C. sauce, and more noodles.
- Continue for all of the ingredients and end with some sauce.
- Cover the dish with foil and cook it all in the oven for 35 mins.
- Enjoy.

Amount per serving (8 total)

Timing Information:

Preparation	30 m
Cooking	2 h
Total Time	2 h 30 m

Nutritional Information:

Calories	511 kcal
Fat	15.8 g
Carbohydrates	69.9g
Protein	32.5 g
Cholesterol	0 mg
Sodium	1074 mg

* Percent Daily Values are based on a 2,000 calorie diet.

Sweet Tofu Stir Fry

Ingredients

- 1 tbsp vegetable oil
- 1/2 medium onion, sliced
- 2 cloves garlic, finely chopped
- 1 tbsp fresh ginger root, finely chopped
- 1 (16 oz.) package tofu, drained and cut into cubes
- 1/2 C. water
- 4 tbsps rice wine vinegar
- 2 tbsps honey
- 2 tbsps soy sauce
- 2 tsps cornstarch dissolved in
- 2 tbsps water
- 1 carrot, peeled and sliced
- 1 green bell pepper, seeded and cut into strips
- 1 C. baby corn, drained and cut into pieces
- 1 small head bok choy, chopped
- 2 C. fresh mushrooms, chopped
- 1 1/4 C. bean sprouts

- 1 C. bamboo shoots, drained and chopped
- 1/2 tsp crushed red pepper
- 2 medium green onions, thinly sliced diagonally

Directions

- Stir fry your onions for 2 mins in oil then add the ginger and garlic.
- Cook this mix for 1 more min before adding the tofu and frying until it has browned.
- Now add the corn, carrots, and bell peppers and cook for 4 more mins then add the red pepper, bok choy, bamboo, mushrooms, and bean sprouts.
- Cook for 1 more min to get everything hot then shut the heat.
- In a smaller pot and get the following simmering with a high level of heat and then a low one: soy sauce, water, honey, and vinegar.

- Simmer for 4 mins then add the water and cornstarch mix.
- Cook the mix until everything becomes a thick sauce.
- Top your tofu with this sauce.
- Now add scallions when serving.
- Enjoy.

Amount per serving (4 total)

Timing Information:

Preparation	30 m
Cooking	15 m
Total Time	45 m

Nutritional Information:

Calories	215 kcal
Fat	9.4 g
Carbohydrates	24g
Protein	13.6 g
Cholesterol	0 mg
Sodium	507 mg

* Percent Daily Values are based on a 2,000 calorie diet.

American Style Tofu

Ingredients

- 3 tbsps butter
- 1 lb firm tofu, sliced into 1/4 inch slices
- 2 C. whole wheat flour
- 1 C. water
- 1/4 C. dry white wine
- 2 cubes vegetable bouillon
- 4 tbsps prepared mustard
- 1/4 C. honey

Directions

- Coat your tofu with flour and fry them in butter.
- Get the tofu browned all over and then add in bouillon, water, and wine.
- Get everything gently boiling and let it go for 12 mins.

- Now finally add in the honey and mustard.
- Enjoy.

Amount per serving (4 total)

Timing Information:

Preparation	5 m
Cooking	20 m
Total Time	25 m

Nutritional Information:

Calories	532 kcal
Fat	20.3 g
Carbohydrates	67.1g
Protein	27 g
Cholesterol	23 mg
Sodium	262 mg

* Percent Daily Values are based on a 2,000 calorie diet.

Tofu Pudding

Ingredients

- 1 C. semisweet chocolate chips
- 2 tbsps water
- 1 (16 oz.) package firm tofu, drained
- 1/4 C. soy milk
- 1 tbsp vanilla extract

Directions

- Melt your chocolate, then puree it with the tofu in a blender, and add in the vanilla and milk.
- Continue pureeing for 2 to 5 mins.
- Place everything in the fridge until cold.
- Enjoy.

Amount per serving (6 total)

Timing Information:

Preparation	
Cooking	10 m
Total Time	10 m

Nutritional Information:

Calories	198 kcal
Fat	11.7 g
Carbohydrates	19.8g
Protein	7.6 g
Cholesterol	0 mg
Sodium	18 mg

* Percent Daily Values are based on a 2,000 calorie diet.

Indian Style Tofu

Ingredients

- 3 tbsps vegetable oil
- 2 inch piece fresh ginger root, peeled and minced
- 2 onions, halved and sliced
- 1/2 head cauliflower, cut into florets
- 3 carrots, peeled and sliced
- 3 tbsps vindaloo curry powder
- 6 tbsps tomato paste
- 1 (15 oz.) can coconut milk
- 1 C. vegetable broth
- 1 (15 oz.) can garbanzo beans (chickpeas), drained and rinsed
- 1 lb extra-firm tofu, cut into 1-inch cubes
- 1 C. mushrooms, sliced
- salt to taste

Directions

- Stir fry your ginger in veggie oil in a big pot for 3 mins then add in: carrots, cauliflower, and onions.
- Cook the mix for about 7 more mins while stirring.
- Now add in the tomato paste, and vindaloo.
- Stir everything evenly and then add: beans, salt, mushrooms, tofu, coconut milk, and broth.
- Get the mix boiling, and then place a lid on the pot, set the heat to low, and let the contents gently boil for 17 mins.
- Enjoy.

Amount per serving (6 total)

Timing Information:

Preparation	25 m
Cooking	35 m
Total Time	1 h

Nutritional Information:

Calories	413 kcal
Fat	27.8 g
Carbohydrates	33.2g
Protein	15.1 g
Cholesterol	0 mg
Sodium	401 mg

* Percent Daily Values are based on a 2,000 calorie diet.

Cilantro and Sesame Tofu

Ingredients

- 1 lb firm tofu, cut into 4 pieces, then cut diagonally, into 8 triangles, pressed and drained
- 1 C. fresh orange juice
- 1/4 C. rice vinegar
- 1/3 C. soy sauce
- 1/3 C. canola oil
- 4 tsps dark sesame oil
- 3 cloves garlic, minced
- 1 tbsp minced fresh ginger root
- 1/4 tsp red pepper flakes
- 1 green onions, cut into 1-inch strips
- 1/4 C. coarsely chopped fresh cilantro
- 2 dried chipotle chili pepper, stems removed, and diced

Directions

- Get a bowl, combine: cilantro, pepper flakes, onions, orange juice, ginger, chilies, vinegar, oils, and soy sauce.
- Layer all your tofu pieces into a casserole dish and top with the orange sauce.
- Place a covering of plastic around the dish and put everything in the fridge for 40 mins.
- Set your oven to 350 degrees before doing anything else.
- Remove about half of the marinade from the dish and cook it all in the oven for 50 mins.
- Enjoy.

Amount per serving (4 total)

Timing Information:

Preparation	
Cooking	25 m
Total Time	1 h 25 m

Nutritional Information:

Calories	419 kcal
Fat	33.6 g
Carbohydrates	14.6g
Protein	20 g
Cholesterol	0 mg
Sodium	1224 mg

* Percent Daily Values are based on a 2,000 calorie diet.

Tofu Party Dip

Ingredients

- 1 lb firm tofu, pressed, drained, and then frozen
- 1 stalk celery, chopped
- 1 green onion, chopped
- 1/2 C. mayonnaise
- 2 tbsps soy sauce
- 1 tbsp lemon juice

Directions

- Take your frozen tofu and thaw it.
- Once the tofu is no longer frozen press out any liquids.
- Add the tofu to a bowl and mash it.
- Combine with the tofu: lemon juice, celery, soy sauce, onions, and mayo.
- Place the mix in the fridge to chill.
- Enjoy.

Amount per serving (4 total)

Timing Information:

Preparation	
Cooking	15 m
Total Time	15 m

Nutritional Information:

Calories	370 kcal
Fat	31.8 g
Carbohydrates	7.2g
Protein	18.8 g
Cholesterol	10 mg
Sodium	632 mg

* Percent Daily Values are based on a 2,000 calorie diet.

3 Cheese Tofu Pasta Shells

Ingredients

- 1 (16 oz.) package jumbo pasta shells
- 1/3 C. grated carrot
- 1/4 C. shredded zucchini
- 3 tbsps chopped onion
- 1 (8 oz.) container tofu
- 1/2 C. shredded Monterey Jack cheese
- 1 C. shredded mozzarella cheese, divided
- 1/2 C. ricotta cheese
- 1 egg white
- 1/2 tsp salt
- 1/2 tsp pepper
- 2 (8 oz.) cans diced tomatoes
- 1/3 C. tomato paste
- 1 tsp dried basil
- 1 tsp dried oregano
- 1/4 tsp garlic powder
- 1 tsp minced garlic

Directions

- Set your oven to 350 degrees before doing anything else.
- Boil your pasta in water and salt for 9 mins. Then remove all the liquid.
- Simultaneously cook your onions, zucchini, and carrots, in water, until soft. Then remove the liquids.
- Get a bowl and crumble your tofu in it.
- Add in: pepper, carrot mix, salt, Monterey, egg, half C. mozzarella, and ricotta.
- Get the following boiling: garlic, tomatoes, garlic powder, tomato paste, oregano, and basil.
- Once everything is boiling reduce the heat and let it cook for 12 mins.
- Fill your pasta with the tofu mix and layer the shells in a casserole dish.

- Top the pasta with the sauce and place a covering of foil around the entire dish.
- Cook everything in the oven for 30 mins.
- Top the pasta with the rest of mozzarella and let it melt for 5 mins.
- Enjoy.

Amount per serving (4 total)

Timing Information:

Preparation	10 m
Cooking	45 m
Total Time	55 m

Nutritional Information:

Calories	688 kcal
Fat	15.8 g
Carbohydrates	98.9g
Protein	36.4 g
Cholesterol	40 mg
Sodium	961 mg

* Percent Daily Values are based on a 2,000 calorie diet.

Cranberry, Pecan, and Pepper Tofu

Ingredients

- 1 1/2 C. brown rice
- 6 large green bell peppers
- 3 tbsps soy sauce
- 3 tbsps cooking sherry
- 1 tsp vegetarian Worcestershire sauce
- 1 1/2 C. extra firm tofu
- 1/2 C. sweetened dried cranberries
- 1/4 C. chopped pecans
- 1/2 C. grated Parmesan cheese
- salt and pepper to taste
- 2 C. tomato sauce
- 2 tbsps brown sugar

Directions

- Set your oven to 350 degrees before doing anything else.

- Get 3 C. of water and your rice boiling, then place a lid on the pot, set the heat to low, and let the rice cook for 42 mins.
- Simultaneously remove the flesh of your pepper and put the shells in a bowl with half an inch of water.
- Cook the peppers for 7 mins in the microwave.
- Get the following boiling: Worcestershire, soy sauce, and wine.
- Once the mix is boiling lower the heat and add the tofu.
- Let the mix lightly boil until all the liquid is gone.
- Get a bowl, mix: pepper, rice, salt, tofu, cheese, cranberries, and nuts.
- Fill your pepper shells evenly with the mix then layer everything in a casserole dish.
- Cook the mix in the oven for 27 mins.

- At the same time heat up some brown sugar and tomato sauce.
- When serving the pepper shells top them with some of the sweet tomato sauce.
- Enjoy.

Amount per serving (6 total)

Timing Information:

Preparation	10 m
Cooking	1 h 10 m
Total Time	1 h 20 m

Nutritional Information:

Calories	375 kcal
Fat	10.2 g
Carbohydrates	59.6g
Protein	14.9 g
Cholesterol	6 mg
Sodium	1055 mg

* Percent Daily Values are based on a 2,000 calorie diet.

German Style Tofu

Ingredients

- 1 (16 oz.) package uncooked egg noodles
- 2 (12 oz.) packages extra-firm tofu, drained and diced
- 1 tbsp vegetable oil
- 2 onions, sliced
- 1 (12 oz.) container cottage cheese
- 2 tbsps sour cream
- 1 sprig fresh dill weed, chopped
- 8 oz. mushrooms, sliced
- 1 tsp garlic, minced
- 2 tbsps soy sauce

Directions

- Boil your noodles for 9 mins in water then remove all the liquids.

- Stir fry your tofu for 7 mins on each side then remove the pieces from the pan.
- Add in the onions and cook them until soft.
- Now add: soy sauce, garlic, and mushrooms.
- Cook the mix until hot for 2 mins.
- Get a bowl, combine: dill, cottage cheese, and sour cream. Add this with the mushrooms and also add in the tofu.
- Cook the mix for 3 more mins.
- Serve the noodles with a topping of tofu mix.
- Enjoy.

Amount per serving (8 total)

Timing Information:

Preparation	15 m
Cooking	30 m
Total Time	45 m

Nutritional Information:

Calories	356 kcal
Fat	12.3 g
Carbohydrates	42.1g
Protein	21.5 g
Cholesterol	49 mg
Sodium	416 mg

* Percent Daily Values are based on a 2,000 calorie diet.

Mushrooms and Pasta Tofu

Ingredients

- 1/2 C. seashell pasta
- 1 C. tomato sauce
- 1/2 C. mushrooms, diced
- 1/4 C. crumbled firm silken tofu
- 1/4 C. shredded mozzarella cheese
- 2 tbsps grated Parmesan cheese

Directions

- Boil your pasta in water and salt for 9 mins then remove all the liquids.
- Set your oven to 400 degrees before doing anything else.
- Get a bowl, mix: pasta, tomato sauce, tofu, and mushrooms.
- Get a 2nd bowl, mix: parmesan and mozzarella.

- Combine both bowls evenly then add everything to a baking dish and cook the contents in the oven for 35 mins.
- Enjoy.

Amount per serving (2 total)

Timing Information:

Preparation	10 m
Cooking	30 m
Total Time	40 m

Nutritional Information:

Calories	212 kcal
Fat	5.5 g
Carbohydrates	29.5g
Protein	13.3 g
Cholesterol	13 mg
Sodium	819 mg

* Percent Daily Values are based on a 2,000 calorie diet.

Choco Tofu Pie

Ingredients

- 1 lb silken tofu
- 1/2 C. unsweetened cocoa powder
- 1 C. white sugar
- 1 tbsp vanilla extract
- 1/2 tsp cider vinegar
- 1 (9 inch) prepared graham cracker crust

Directions

- Set your oven to 375 degrees before doing anything else.
- Get a bowl and crumble your tofu in it.
- Then add in: vinegar, cocoa, vanilla, and sugar.
- Get an electric mixer and combine the mix for a few mins.

- Add the contents into the cracker crust and then cook everything in the oven for 27 mins.
- After cooking the dish place it in the fridge for 2 hours.
- Enjoy.

Amount per serving (8 total)

Timing Information:

Preparation	15 m
Cooking	25 m
Total Time	40 m

Nutritional Information:

Calories	293 kcal
Fat	9.7 g
Carbohydrates	49.2g
Protein	5 g
Cholesterol	0 mg
Sodium	175 mg

* Percent Daily Values are based on a 2,000 calorie diet.

Easy Asian Tofu

Ingredients

- 1 (12 oz.) package extra firm tofu, pressed, drained, cubed
- 3 tbsps cornstarch
- oil for frying
- 2 green onions, chopped
- 2 tbsps hoisin sauce

Directions

- Get a bowl and add in your cornstarch.
- Now evenly coat all your tofu cubes with it.
- For 5 mins per side fry your tofu in oil then top it with green onions and hoisin sauce.
- Enjoy.

Amount per serving (2 total)

Timing Information:

Preparation	10 m
Cooking	5 m
Total Time	15 m

Nutritional Information:

Calories	433 kcal
Fat	32.4 g
Carbohydrates	22.5g
Protein	17.5 g
Cholesterol	1 mg
Sodium	275 mg

* Percent Daily Values are based on a 2,000 calorie diet.

Tofu Salad II

Ingredients

- 1 tbsp sweet chili sauce
- 1/2 tsp grated fresh ginger root
- 2 cloves garlic, crushed
- 1 tbsp dark soy sauce
- 1 tbsp sesame oil
- 1/2 (16 oz.) package extra-firm tofu, drained and diced
- 1 C. snow peas, trimmed
- 2 small carrots, grated
- 1 C. finely shredded red cabbage
- 2 tbsps chopped peanuts

Directions

- Get a bowl, combine: sesame oil, chili sauce, soy sauce, ginger, tofu, and garlic.
- Place a covering over the bowl and put it all in the fridge for 2 hrs.

- Boil your peas in water for 3 mins then run them under cold water with a strainer.
- Take out the tofu after 2 hrs has elapsed and combine in: peanuts, peas, cabbage, and carrots.
- Enjoy.

Amount per serving (4 total)

Timing Information:

Preparation	15 m
Cooking	2 m
Total Time	1 h 20 m

Nutritional Information:

Calories	145 kcal
Fat	9.1 g
Carbohydrates	10.1g
Protein	8.2 g
Cholesterol	0 mg
Sodium	295 mg

* Percent Daily Values are based on a 2,000 calorie diet.

Triple Tofu Quiche II

Ingredients

- 1 (9 inch) unbaked 9 inch pie crust
- 1 lb broccoli, chopped
- 1 tbsp olive oil
- 1 onion, finely chopped
- 4 cloves garlic, minced
- 1 lb firm tofu, drained
- 1/2 C. soy milk
- 1/4 tsp Dijon mustard
- 3/4 tsp salt
- 1/4 tsp ground nutmeg
- 1/2 tsp ground red pepper
- black pepper to taste
- 1 tbsp dried parsley
- 1/8 C. Parmesan flavor soy cheese

Directions

- Set your oven to 400 degrees before doing anything else.
- Now bake the pie crust for 15 mins.
- Steam your broccoli over 2 inches of boiling water, with a steamer insert, in a big pot, for 7 mins, then remove all the liquids.
- Now stir fry your garlic and onions until browned and then combine in the broccoli and heat it up.
- Puree the following in a blender: parmesan, tofu, parsley, milk, black pepper, mustard, red pepper, nutmeg, and salt.
- Get a bowl, combine: broccoli and the tofu mix.
- Now fill the crust with the mix and cook the pie in the oven for 37 mins.
- Enjoy.

Amount per serving (6 total)

Timing Information:

Preparation	20 m
Cooking	40 m
Total Time	1 h 5 m

Nutritional Information:

Calories	337 kcal
Fat	19.6 g
Carbohydrates	26.3g
Protein	18 g
Cholesterol	0 mg
Sodium	532 mg

* Percent Daily Values are based on a 2,000 calorie diet.

Peppers and Mozzarella Tofu

Ingredients

- 1 C. uncooked brown rice
- 2 C. water
- 2 tbsps olive oil
- 1 clove garlic, minced
- 1 (12 oz.) package extra-firm tofu, drained and diced
- 1 3/4 C. marinara sauce, divided
- salt to taste
- ground black pepper to taste
- 2 red bell peppers, halved and seeded
- 2 orange bell peppers, halved and seeded
- 2 C. shredded mozzarella cheese
- 8 slices tomato

Directions

- Get your water and rice boiling, then place a lid on the pot, set the heat to low, and let the rice cook for 47 mins.
- Stir fry your tofu and garlic in olive oil for 7 mins then add a quarter of a C. of marinara, pepper, and salt.
- Cook the mix for 5 more mins.
- Now set your oven to 350 degrees before doing anything else.
- Divide your rice amongst your peppers and top everything with the rest of the marinara and half of your cheese.
- Divide the tofu mix amongst the pepper shells and press it all together.
- Finally top the peppers with the rest of the cheese.
- Layer everything into a casserole dish and cook the contents in the oven for 30 mins.
- Enjoy.

Amount per serving (4 total)

Timing Information:

Preparation	25 m
Cooking	1 h 10 m
Total Time	1 h 35 m

Nutritional Information:

Calories	554 kcal
Fat	25 g
Carbohydrates	56.1g
Protein	28.5 g
Cholesterol	38 mg
Sodium	813 mg

* Percent Daily Values are based on a 2,000 calorie diet.

Indian Style Tofu II

Ingredients

- 1 (16 oz.) package firm tofu, pressed, drained, and then freeze for 8 hrs
- 3 tbsps vegetable oil
- 1 tsp cumin seeds
- 1 onion, chopped
- 1 tsp minced fresh ginger root
- 1 tsp minced garlic
- 1 C. frozen peas, thawed
- 2 tsps curry powder
- 1 C. chopped fresh tomatoes
- salt to taste
- 1 fresh jalapeno pepper, chopped

Directions

- Thaw out your tofu then mash it.
- Fry your cumin seeds in oil until they begin sputter then add in: garlic, onions, and ginger.

- Cook this mix for 1 more min before adding: curry powder, tofu, and peas.
- Now continue frying for 7 more mins.
- Add the salt and tomatoes.
- Place a lid on the pan and let the contents cook for 17 mins with a low level of heat.
- Finally add the chopped pepper and cook for 4 more mins before plating the contents.
- Enjoy.

Amount per serving (4 total)

Timing Information:

Preparation	15 m
Cooking	25 m
Total Time	40 m

Nutritional Information:

Calories	340 kcal
Fat	21.8 g
Carbohydrates	20.2g
Protein	21.4 g
Cholesterol	0 mg
Sodium	547 mg

* Percent Daily Values are based on a 2,000 calorie diet.

Rice and Spinach Tofu

Ingredients

- 2 C. uncooked sushi (sticky) or medium-grain rice
- 4 C. water
- 2/3 C. peanut butter
- 1 C. hot water
- 2 tbsps soy sauce
- 2 tbsps rice vinegar
- 3 tbsps white sugar
- 3 cloves garlic, minced
- 3 green onions, chopped
- 1/4 tsp red pepper flakes
- 1 (10 oz.) bag baby spinach leaves
- 1 (8 oz.) package baked tofu, cut into bite-size pieces

Directions

- Get your water (4 C.) and rice boiling, then place a lid on the

- pot, set the heat to low, and let the contents cook for 22 mins.
- Meanwhile add the following to a pan and get it simmering: red pepper flakes, peanut butter, green onions, hot water (1 C.), garlic, soy sauce, sugar, and vinegar.
- Simmer this mix while the rice cooks and then add in some water (1/4 C.) to keep it sauce-like.
- Get 2 inches of water boiling and cook your spinach and the tofu with a steamer insert.
- Let the tofu and spinach cook for 9 mins with a cover on the pot.
- Layer the rice on a serving plate, then some spinach, and then a liberal amount of sauce.
- Enjoy.

Amount per serving (4 total)

Timing Information:

Preparation	10 m
Cooking	40 m
Total Time	1 h

Nutritional Information:

Calories	749 kcal
Fat	27.5 g
Carbohydrates	100.2g
Protein	29 g
Cholesterol	0 mg
Sodium	1002 mg

* Percent Daily Values are based on a 2,000 calorie diet.

Peanut Butter and Ginger Tofu

Ingredients

- 2 tbsps rice vinegar
- 2 tbsps ketchup
- 2 tbsps peanut butter
- 1 tsp low-sodium soy sauce
- 1 tsp sesame oil
- 1 clove garlic, minced
- 1/2 tsp ground ginger
- 1/4 tsp cayenne pepper, or to taste
- fresh ground black pepper
- 1 (16 oz.) package extra-firm tofu, cut into 1/2-inch cubes

Directions

- Get a bowl, combine: black pepper, vinegar, cayenne, ketchup, ginger, peanut butter,

garlic, sesame oil, and soy sauce.
- Cook the mix for 1 min in the microwave and then stir it.
- Add in the tofu and toss the mix to coat evenly.
- Place a covering around the bowl and place it in the fridge for 1 hr.
- Now set your oven to 400 degrees before doing anything else.
- Layer all your tofu pieces and the marinade in a casserole dish and cook everything in the oven for 17 mins.
- Enjoy.

Amount per serving (6 total)

Timing Information:

Preparation	10 m
Cooking	10 m
Total Time	50 m

Nutritional Information:

Calories	114 kcal
Fat	7.9 g
Carbohydrates	4.3g
Protein	8.9 g
Cholesterol	0 mg
Sodium	116 mg

* Percent Daily Values are based on a 2,000 calorie diet.

Easy Japanese Style Tofu

Ingredients

- 1 (12 oz.) package firm tofu, pressed, drained, diced
- 1 C. chopped fresh pineapple
- 1 C. teriyaki sauce

Directions

- Get a bowl, combine: teriyaki sauce, tofu, and pineapple.
- Place everything in the fridge for 2 hrs then pour the contents into a casserole dish.
- Set your oven to 350 degrees before anything else and cook the tofu in the oven for 25 mins.
- Enjoy.

Amount per serving (4 total)

Timing Information:

Preparation	10 m
Cooking	20 m
Total Time	1 d 1 h 30

Nutritional Information:

Calories	272 kcal
Fat	7.5 g
Carbohydrates	31.5g
Protein	22.2 g
Cholesterol	0 mg
Sodium	5532 mg

* Percent Daily Values are based on a 2,000 calorie diet.

Tofu Chili

Ingredients

- 1/2 (12 oz.) package extra firm tofu
- 1 tsp chili powder
- 1 clove garlic, minced
- 2 tbsps vegetable oil
- 1/2 C. onion, chopped
- 2 stalks celery, chopped
- 1/2 C. whole kernel corn, undrained
- 1 (15.25 oz.) can kidney beans, undrained
- 1 (14.5 oz.) can stewed tomatoes, undrained
- 1 quart water

Directions

- Get a bowl, mash: garlic, tofu, and chili powder.

- Stir fry your celery and onions in oil until soft then add in the tofu mix.
- Continue stir frying for 7 mins then add: tomatoes, corn, and beans.
- Get everything boiling and then add in the water and get it all boiling again.
- Set the heat to low and let the chili cook for 60 mins.
- Enjoy.

Amount per serving (8 total)

Timing Information:

Preparation	15 m
Cooking	1 h
Total Time	1 h 15 m

Nutritional Information:

Calories	123 kcal
Fat	5.1 g
Carbohydrates	15.2g
Protein	5.9 g
Cholesterol	0 mg
Sodium	275 mg

* Percent Daily Values are based on a 2,000 calorie diet.

Taiwanese Style Tofu

Ingredients

- 1 (16 oz.) package extra firm tofu, pressed, drained, cut in half lengthwise, then into 4 rectangular pieces
- 1/3 C. soy sauce
- 2 tsps Chinese black vinegar
- 1 tsp sesame oil
- 1 tsp white sugar
- 3 tbsps olive oil
- 3 cloves garlic, minced
- 1/4 C. chopped green onions
- salt and pepper to taste

Directions

- Get a bowl, combine: sugar, soy sauce, sesame oil, and vinegar.
- Stir fry your onions and garlic for 1 min then add the tofu and get it browned all over. Add in the

vinegar mix and cook everything for 5 mins.
- Finally add in your preferred amount of pepper and salt.
- Enjoy.

Amount per serving (5 total)

Timing Information:

Preparation	20 m
Cooking	10 m
Total Time	30 m

Nutritional Information:

Calories	230 kcal
Fat	17 g
Carbohydrates	7.3g
Protein	15.6 g
Cholesterol	0 mg
Sodium	1093 mg

* Percent Daily Values are based on a 2,000 calorie diet.

Tofu Tartar Sandwich

Ingredients

- 1 (12 oz.) package firm tofu - drained, patted dry, and sliced into 4 slices
- 1 C. bread crumbs
- 1 tsp kelp powder
- 1/4 tsp garlic powder
- 1/4 tsp paprika
- 1/4 tsp onion powder or flakes
- 1 tsp salt
- olive oil, as needed

Tartar Sauce:
- 1/2 C. mayonnaise
- 1/4 C. dill pickle relish
- 1 tbsp fresh lemon juice
- 4 whole wheat hamburger buns, split

Directions

- Set your oven to 350 degrees before doing anything else.
- Get a bowl, combine: salt, bread crumbs, onions powder, kelp, paprika, and garlic powder.
- Coat your tofu pieces with some olive oil then dredge them in the dry mix.
- Place everything in a casserole dish and cook it all in the oven for 35 mins.
- Flip the pieces half way through the cooking time.
- At the same time as the tofu cooks get a bowl, and combine: lemon juice, mayo, and relish.
- Coat your bread with the mayo mix liberally then add some tofu and also some tartar.
- Enjoy.

Amount per serving (4 total)

Timing Information:

Preparation	15 m
Cooking	30 m
Total Time	45 m

Nutritional Information:

Calories	622 kcal
Fat	41.6 g
Carbohydrates	43.7g
Protein	21.4 g
Cholesterol	11 mg
Sodium	1332 mg

* Percent Daily Values are based on a 2,000 calorie diet.

Caribbean Style Tofu

Ingredients

- 1 1/2 C. water
- 1 C. uncooked basmati rice, rinsed and drained
- 3 tbsps sesame oil
- 1 (14 oz.) package firm water-packed tofu, drained and cubed
- 1/4 tsp salt
- 1 (10 oz.) can coconut milk
- 2 tbsps green curry paste

Directions

- Get your rice and water boiling then place a lid on the pot, set the heat to low, and let the rice cook for 22 mins.
- Once it has cooled off a bit stir it.
- Fry your tofu in sesame oil for 20 mins while stirring and use a medium to low level of heat.

- Then add some salt and pepper.
- Get your coconut milk boiling in a separate pan then add in: curry paste and set the heat to low and gently boil for 7 mins.
- Layer your rice on a serving plate then top it with the tofu and liberally with curry coconut sauce.
- Enjoy

Amount per serving (4 total)

Timing Information:

Preparation	20 m
Cooking	25 m
Total Time	45 m

Nutritional Information:

Calories	536 kcal
Fat	37.9 g
Carbohydrates	44.2g
Protein	23.2 g
Cholesterol	0 mg
Sodium	312 mg

* Percent Daily Values are based on a 2,000 calorie diet.

Easy Tofu Cheesecake

Ingredients

- 2 (12 oz.) packages extra firm tofu, drained and cubed
- 1 C. white sugar
- 1 tsp vanilla extract
- 1/4 tsp salt
- 1/4 C. vegetable oil
- 2 tbsps lemon juice
- 1 (9 inch) prepared graham cracker crust

Directions

- Set your oven to 350 degrees before doing anything else.
- Puree: lemon juice, tofu, veggie oil, sugar, salt, and vanilla.
- Fill your crust with the puree and cook it in the oven for 25 mins.
- Now place the pie in the fridge until cold.

- Enjoy.

Amount per serving (8 total)

Timing Information:

Preparation	10 m
Cooking	20 m
Total Time	2 h 30 m

Nutritional Information:

Calories	371 kcal
Fat	18.3 g
Carbohydrates	46.4g
Protein	8.1 g
Cholesterol	0 mg
Sodium	249 mg

* Percent Daily Values are based on a 2,000 calorie diet.

Ranch and Spinach Tofu

Ingredients

- 2 (10 inch) whole wheat tortillas
- 1 (7.5 oz.) package hickory flavor baked tofu
- 1/2 C. shredded sharp Cheddar cheese
- 1 C. fresh baby spinach
- 1 tbsp Ranch dressing
- 1 tbsp grated Parmesan cheese, or to taste

Directions

- Cut your tofu into strips and evenly divide the strips amongst your tortillas along with some cheddar. Microwave for 1 mins.
- Now add some ranch and spinach to each tortilla and finally parmesan.
- Form a wrap and then serve.

- Enjoy.

Amount per serving (2 total)

Timing Information:

Preparation	3 m
Cooking	2 m
Total Time	5 m

Nutritional Information:

Calories	449 kcal
Fat	20.4 g
Carbohydrates	33.9g
Protein	35.2 g
Cholesterol	40 mg
Sodium	567 mg

* Percent Daily Values are based on a 2,000 calorie diet.

Indian Style Tofu III

Ingredients

- 1 (16 oz.) package tofu
- 1/2 C. plain yogurt
- 2 tbsps lemon juice
- 2 tsps ground cumin
- 1/2 tsp cayenne pepper
- 1 tsp paprika
- 1 tsp garam masala
- 1 tbsp minced fresh ginger root
- 2 tbsps unsalted butter
- 4 cloves garlic, minced
- 3 serrano peppers, seeded and minced
- 4 tsps ground coriander
- 2 tsps ground cumin
- 2 tsps garam masala
- 1/2 tsp salt
- 1 (16 oz.) can tomato sauce
- 1 small head cauliflower, cut into florets
- 2 C. half-and-half cream
- 1 C. frozen peas

- 1/4 C. chopped fresh cilantro

Directions

- Put your tofu between two plates and place a skillet on top of one plate to apply pressure on the tofu and help it drain.
- Drain the tofu in this manner for 40 mins.
- Set your oven to 375 degrees before doing anything else.
- Cut the tofu into half an inch cubes.
- Get a bowl, combine: ginger, yogurt, half of your masala, lemon juice, paprika, tofu, cumin, and cayenne.
- Evenly distribute your tofu throughout a cookie sheet and cook them in the oven for 1 hour. Turn the tofu pieces every 20 mins.
- Simultaneously stir fry your serrano peppers and garlic in butter for 4 mins than add: cumin

(2 tsps), remaining masala, coriander and salt.
- Cook for one for min then pour in your tomato sauce and cauliflower.
- Place a lid on the pan and then let the contents simmer for 17 mins.
- Now add in the half and half, peas, tofu, and cilantro. Cook for 7 more mins.
- Enjoy with basmati rice.

Amount per serving (4 total)

Timing Information:

Preparation	20 m
Cooking	50 m
Total Time	1 h 30 m

Nutritional Information:

Calories	421 kcal
Fat	27.3 g
Carbohydrates	30g
Protein	20.5 g
Cholesterol	62 mg
Sodium	1038 mg

* Percent Daily Values are based on a 2,000 calorie diet.

California Style Tofu

Ingredients

- 1 (8 oz.) container extra firm tofu, drained and sliced into large chunks
- 1 zucchini, cut into large chunks
- 1 red bell pepper, cut into large chunks
- 10 large mushrooms
- 2 tbsps sriracha chili garlic sauce
- 1/4 C. soy sauce
- 2 tbsps sesame oil
- 1/4 C. diced onion
- 1 jalapeno pepper, diced
- ground black pepper to taste

Directions

- Get a bowl, combine: mushrooms, bell peppers, zucchini, and tofu.

- Get a 2nd bowl, mix: pepper, sriracha, jalapenos, soy sauce, onions, and sesame oil.
- Combine both bowls then place a covering over it and put it all in the fridge for 60 mins.
- Get your grill hot and ready for cooking.
- Get the grate ready by brushing it with oil.
- Take some skewers and make kebabs from your tofu mix.
- Cook the kebabs for 12 mins on the grill and brush the tofu with more marinade.
- Enjoy.

Amount per serving (2 total)

Timing Information:

Preparation	15 m
Cooking	10 m
Total Time	1 h 25 m

Nutritional Information:

Calories	301 kcal
Fat	19.8 g
Carbohydrates	19.4g
Protein	16.8 g
Cholesterol	0 mg
Sodium	2466 mg

* Percent Daily Values are based on a 2,000 calorie diet.

Olives and Soy Sauce Tofu

Ingredients

- 1 tbsp olive oil, or as needed
- 1 onion, chopped
- 1 (12 oz.) package extra-firm tofu, drained and cubed
- 1/2 (15 oz.) can black olives, drained and halved
- 3 cloves garlic, minced
- 3 tbsps nutritional yeast
- 1 tbsp tamari (dark soy sauce)

Directions

- Stir fry your onions for 12 mins in olive oil and then combine in: garlic, olives, and tofu.
- Place a lid on the pan and cook the tofu for 9 mins then add in your tamari and yeast.
- Cook the mix for 4 more mins before serving.

- Enjoy.

Amount per serving (4 total)

Timing Information:

Preparation	10 m
Cooking	15 m
Total Time	25 m

Nutritional Information:

Calories	190 kcal
Fat	13.3 g
Carbohydrates	10.3g
Protein	11.1 g
Cholesterol	0 mg
Sodium	718 mg

* Percent Daily Values are based on a 2,000 calorie diet.

Pad Thai Noodles

Ingredients

- 2/3 cup dried rice vermicelli
- 1/4 cup peanut oil
- 2/3 cup thinly sliced firm tofu
- 1 large egg, beaten
- 4 cloves garlic, finely chopped
- 1/4 cup vegetable broth
- 2 tbsps fresh lime juice
- 2 tbsps soy sauce
- 1 tbsp white sugar
- 1 tsp salt
- 1/2 tsp dried red chili flakes
- 3 tbsps chopped peanuts
- 1 pound bean sprouts, divided
- 3 green onions, whites cut thinly across and greens sliced into thin lengths - divided
- 3 tbsps chopped peanuts
- 2 limes, cut into wedges for garnish

Directions

- Put rice vermicelli noodles in hot water for about 30 minutes before draining the water.
- Cook tofu in hot oil until golden brown before draining it with paper tower.
- Reserve 1 tbsp of oil for later use and cook egg in the remaining hot oil until done, and set them aside for later use.
- Now cook noodles and garlic in the hot reserved oil, while coating them well with this oil along the way.
- In this pan containing noodles; add tofu, salt, chili flakes, egg and 3 tbsps peanuts, and mix all this very thoroughly.
- Also add bean sprouts and green onion into it, while reserving some for the garnishing purposes.
- Cook all this for two minutes before transferring to a serving platter.

- Garnish this with peanuts and the reserved vegetables before placing some lime wedges around the platter to make this dish more attractive.
- Serve.

Serving: 4

Timing Information:

Preparation	10 m
Cooking	30 m
Total Time	1 h

Nutritional Information:

Calories	397 kcal
Carbohydrates	39.5 g
Cholesterol	41 mg
Fat	23.3 g
Fiber	5 g
Protein	13.2 g
Sodium	1234 mg

* Percent Daily Values are based on a 2,000 calorie diet.

Thanks for Reading! Now Let's try some Sushi and Dump Dinners....

http://bit.ly/2443TFg

To grab this **box set** simply follow the link mentioned above, or tap the book cover.

This will take you to a page where you can simply enter your email address and a PDF version of the **box set** will be emailed to you.

I hope you are ready for some serious cooking!

http://bit.ly/2443TFg

You will also receive updates about all my new books when they are free.

Also don't forget to like and subscribe on the social networks. I love meeting my readers. Links to all my profiles are below so please click and connect :)

[Facebook](#)

[Twitter](#)

Made in the USA
Las Vegas, NV
08 January 2022